HIP HOP APPS

"Making PEOPLE GREAT Again"
A Parent's Guide to starting your child's career!

by

DERWIN C. JORDAN

TABLE OF CONTENTS

Acknowledgements

To name the number of people that have touched my career over the years would be its very own novel. I would like to thank Melissa Dean for helping me edit this book and put up with my many emails and text messages to get this project off the ground. I would like to thank my daughter's *Jasmine, Morgan, Taylor, and Isabella* for being such an amazing example of what students, employees and daughters should be. This book is dedicated to them. In the hope that they will continue to be amazing examples in Bible Class, School, and throughout their career. I love you all, and thank you from the bottom of my heart.

Love, Dad

Chapter One

Should your child be working?

Hello my name is Derwin Coryell Jordan. I have been working in the restaurant and entertainment industry for over 25 years now. I'm writing this book because I have had such an amazing opportunity in the choice of my employers. This will be a short read, as my main goal is for you to examine how your child is performing in the work place. The most important question you must ask is "Should my child be working while they are in school?" This is a question most parents don't ask, or they don't have this much-needed conversation with their children prior to sending them off into the workforce. First and foremost, it is very rare that a company will only employ people who are between the ages of 16-18 years old. To have employees that can work during the time your child is in school, companies often hire several young, middle aged, and even in some cases elderly adults. I would venture to say that if a probe was done, you would be very shocked to learn that even greater than the number of school teachers who are getting caught up in sexual relationships with students, is the number of teenagers that are dating people far beyond their age in the workforce. (We will cover that in "What is HR and how does it relate to my child".) In addition to the question of age, a parent should ask "What activities does your child participate in at school?" The biggest obstacle to retention of high school employees is attendance. I repeat, the BIGGEST problem with retention of high school aged employees is their attendance.

Therefore, prior to your child getting a job, you should discuss the hours that they are available to work. If you are a family that goes on vacation during the holidays, it is likely that your child should not get a job, or you should plan on your child working during this time. Most jobs that employ high school students are often at the peak of their business during the holidays. Every single employer understands that school is your child's number one priority. So, if your child is struggling with grades, it's likely that he or she should get a job that allows them to work only on weekends and holidays, or wait to have your child work when school is not in session. Employers also know that if school is number one, then church is number two. Or vice versa. Surely they understand that all families go to church or have some form of religious commitment on Sundays. However, if you are not willing to allow your child to work at all on Sunday, and he or she is extremely limited in their availability during the week, it is likely that your child is not ready to enter the workforce.

The next conversation you should have with your child is about their priorities and what they need to do to ensure they remain productive both at school and at work. Needing to be off Saturday evenings because your son usually skateboards with the neighborhood kids is not a valid reason to be off. An important church choir rehearsal is a pretty good reason to miss work, but again you must assess your child's responsibilities that may potentially limit their ability to work and then decide if they should be working or not. There are a ton of employees who need limited part time work. But you must be sure that your child's priorities are set with very reasonable expectations. Over the years I've seen so many young people come into work after football, basketball, and especially band practice beat to a pulp. Their energy is low and consequently, their productivity is abysmal. Considering this will be the foundation for building their life in the job force, it is critical that you teach them the importance of not just looking at this as sneaker money. Today's cost for toys and things that our children enjoy has gone up substantially. I remember as a child wanting a Nintendo Entertainment System. The cost was $199.00. It was several months away from Christmas and after playing one at my best friend Lamont Gregory's house, I just had to have one. With an allowance of $25 per week, it took me 2 months of sacrificing money for fun to get my system. The Atari system that I'd been playing over the previous 5 years just wasn't the same anymore. As a reward, my grandmother purchased my first game Double Dribble, and I wouldn't go outside for weeks. The point here is not to lose focus that there should be some reward for their efforts to be a contributing member of the workforce. As parents, in the beginning, (Parental Genesis 1:1), we provide EVERYTHING for our children. Even before they can form the words to ask, we provide them with the sustenance they need to survive, the clothes they need to stay warm, and the mental and physical stimulation they need to grow. But once they start to approach puberty, as parents, we need to start teaching them to make the right decisions. We must remember that if they are not making mistakes, they are not making decisions. So, we must also, as parents, understand that it is our RESPONSIBILITY to form our children's opinion of the workforce. (We will discuss this further in "People don't leave companies, they leave manager's.") Bearing this in mind, it is instrumental that you filter frustrations with YOUR problems in the workforce. Often our children will form preconceived notions of how to treat their employers by how they hear YOU at home saying you treat yours. We all must admit that the way we speak at home about our job situation is often different from how we behave in the work place. This is because at home we are more willing to say the things that we want to say at work. But when at work we understand and remember the necessity of being able to feed our children and pay our bills. Therefore, because you are helping to shape your child's opinion of the workplace, they should absolutely understand the need to

REWARD themselves with something when they get paid. Just make sure you are having the conversation about the need to have both a savings and a checking account. Once they start receiving paychecks, teaching them about credit ratings and banking is extremely important. Depending on how well they are maintaining their checking and savings accounts, getting them a local department store credit card would also get them a jump start on establishing their credit score, especially as they get ready to graduate. Once you understand these few basic principles, you can assess whether you as a parent are ready to help people be great again, starting with your very own children.

Now you should begin researching the companies that your child should apply to. Understanding your child's abilities is key here. If your child is not doing their chores at home, is sassy with adults, and doesn't like being told what to do, you have some work to do before they go into the work force. It starts with culture and ends with culture. If you have not instilled Respect, Integrity, and Hard Work in your child, he or she may not be successful in the work place. If your child hates cutting the grass in the summer, getting a job at the local Kroger retrieving the shopping carts outside, is likely not the best career choice. Notice I said career. Never let your child think of their time as an investment into nothing. Don't let them belittle an opportunity to learn any type of trade.

There are also several companies that offer scholarships to young adults who work during their high school years. I received a $1000 scholarship from Chick Fil A upon graduating. I will remember this moment for the rest of my life. Because I was working part time, and God Bless Jesse Chaluh for his patience with scheduling me around being a drum major in the band. With all my extra-curricular activities, it took me an extra summer to retrieve the hours needed for my Chick Fil A scholarship. I remember vividly walking into the financial aid office to apply this check to my student bill. The cashier notified me that my financial grant had arrived, and she took 8 shiny new $100 bills out of the cash register and started counting them. Surely, she was just putting this aside to place in an envelope to send off to some different department. BUT NO, she slid them under the glass and handed me my Paid Fee Receipt. At that very moment, all the cuts from squeezing lemons, staying with my boss Jesse Chaluh at the mall during a tropical storm to feed the employees from Montgomery Ward and JC Penney who were not allowed to close their stores without corporate approval, to the amount of time I cleaned the dining room making sure that the THANK YOU signs on the garbage cans never had ketchup stains, to the long hours of standing while I handed free samples to the people walking by, all flashed before my eyes, and I WAS GRATEFUL. ☺ So, there are benefits to your child working. But remember, attendance is the number one problem with teenaged workers. Making them quit with no notice because of a report card, or making quitting a job punishment, sends the wrong message and burns bridges that could hurt your child down the road. I've seen too many times, young people quit a job during their young years, and fall on hard times wanting to come back. But unfortunately, the way they chose to leave limits their ability in the future to return. Understanding that managers come and go and move around, you never know when you will apply to a job somewhere where they may remember you as a worker at another career of choice. So be a part of the decision, and partner with their development.

Chapter Two

You don't work here....

Some of us have had the joy of working for some AMAZING companies. After spending 14 years with the company that I feel helped form me first into a Gentleman, and then a manager (Dave and Buster's) the number one thing I had to realize after moving on to Incredible Pizza Company, was that they were NOT Dave and Buster's. Chick Fil A set a phenomenal foundation of customer service, and is still leading the workforce in doing so today, but after making it to the 3rd company in my career, I'd learned a valuable lesson. I learned that although the goals were the same at each place I worked, the cultures were much different. They all wanted to take extremely great care of their guests, but how they achieved that goal was quite different. I remember going through the Super Bowl of Service with Chick Fil A. Holiday shopping was our opportunity to serve the people that were out spending their hard-earned money for others. I remember the executives of the company in chicken suits rapping to a Run DMC song pumping us up for the busiest season of the year. Even then we were working on ways to serve our guests with a smile, and serve them QUICKLY. We increased our customer service by making sure that we had sackers, just like the grocery store and allowing the cashiers to just take orders and make sodas. After 4 years of working with the great Jesse Chaluh, I went from the guy who always cleaned the dining room, to assistant night manager. As I became a part of these great organizations, I achieved success by not forgetting the knowledge I learned from the previous employer, but putting it aside to be able to learn 100% of what the ***new investor in my career*** wanted to teach me about their goals and expectations. Once you have assessed your child's ability to work, and measured their performance at home in relation to their ability to be great in the workplace, **YOU, Their Parent, DOES NOT WORK THERE.** Unless you work at the same place that your child is working, you do not know the goals and expectations of their employer.

Remember earlier when I talked about what you say regarding your job at home is often said in a venting manor? In relation, your child's ability to accept constructive criticism in the work place is key. They should learn to welcome feedback, but also understand that they must go in to work with the mindset that they are going to be the best that they can be. They should understand that being on time is being early and being on time is being late. They should take pride in their appearance. If your child is going to school, church, or out on a date looking better than they do going to work, they should not be surprised when they get sent home because they arrived at work with a shirt they pulled out of their locker at school. This chapter may sound a bit harsh, and I must admit that this may be a little form of venting on my part, but as a parent you must understand that you are your child's mentor and manager at home not at the work place. I can't tell you how many times a parent has come up to "ADDRESS" how their baby was being treated, and their "BABY" was the lowest performer on the staff and about to be terminated. Most of these employees did an excellent job during the interview, but once they got the job, it was seen only as an opportunity to hang around their friends who, before your "BABY" came on board, were good employees. Now they only come back from break on time if we send them separately. Or perhaps, they don't show up for work if they request a day off and it's denied. Most of the time they don't even request the day off, or they will wait until the last minute to request the day off and the schedule is already written. You see there is a little system in most places of employment where they go on a first come, first serve day off system. But every now and then, you run across a day like, I don't know, say Christmas. No one wants to work it, and if your child is new, he or she will draw the short end of the stick. But instead of paying their dues, they just don't show up, or call out sick. These things I've mentioned aren't such a big deal when they happen several months apart. In some cases, where the managers aren't holding the underperforming employees accountable, your child may end up surviving these issues, and may even make a rebound and start doing well. But, they may then start to wonder what is holding them up from getting a promotion or a raise. If you establish attendance as the foundation, all they must do to succeed is come to work and do their best, with an amazing attitude, and a willingness to follow guidelines. Even with all of this in place, several parents still manage to miss the boat as it pertains to helping develop their children. Rushing up to your child's place of employment will NOT solve ANYTHING. In fact, it places your child in a category of failure. First and foremost, most companies have a policy that prohibits employers from talking to anyone other than the employee. Also, don't let your child only tell you about the bad things at work. You should have an ongoing conversation with your child about their performance. They need to take ownership of their uniform. If this is their first job, finance them placing their uniform in the cleaners or help them purchase additional uniforms. Companies often issue one or two shirts. If your child is in school, they don't often wash their uniforms soon enough before their next shift. Assist them in learning to be better prepared for their job. In assessing their availability, you should also teach them how to factor in how much time they need to get to work. I don't know what I was more anxious for, working my first shift, or getting my first automobile. There are some very specific questions, and details that the employers want you to know up front, starting with their expectation for your child to work holidays. You should teach them about the application process. Starting with TELL THE TRUTH. Stating in their availability that they can be at work by 4pm, and they get out of school at 3:15pm, and they go to school located 45 minutes from the job location is the recipe for disaster. Particularly if they are in sports or band, you should always have at least a full hour to an hour and a half to get to work. Practices, especially during competition season, playoffs, etc., tend to run longer than usual. But you should also remember things such as the fact that many kids fail to eat at school. Your child should have time to shower, change clothes, do hair/homework, and grab a bite to eat before going to work. Coming straight to work from football/band practice can result in your child having a hygiene problem at work. Often they won't get a break working a 4 or 5-hour shift during the week. Believe it or not, hunger leads to your child doing some very unacceptable things that can lead to termination such as low production, or eating food without permission. Remember that little word I mentioned earlier? INTEGRITY? The second biggest thing that leads to termination for young kids is Theft. (We will cover this more in the "Your Child the hired Hook Up" Chapter)

Chapter 3

People don't leave companies,

they leave manager's!

Most companies have done major research regarding the expectations of their management team, especially as it relates to fraternization policies. I remember the culture of Dave and Buster's was centered around "Ladies and Gentlemen Serving Ladies and Gentlemen." If you have ever worked there you know that there is a very deep separation from employees hanging out with managers. Mainly because it becomes extremely hard to manage the same people you are chugging Jager bombs with at the local Dive Bar. Your child should always make sure they are following the guidelines and goals set forth by the company. They should be careful not to give anyone excuses to speak of them as anything other than a ray of sunshine. It is important that you teach your child to learn the chain of command. Often, new employees look at the top manager in the building and try to look busy anytime the boss come around. But, it is often not this manager that your child should be showing their best to. This explains why most Regional/Area managers often return to evaluate the store after the General Manager leaves for the day, or they may show up unannounced to dodge the dog and pony show. It is important that your child is consistent with their performance on every shift they work. Remember I said it is important for us to form our child's opinion of what the workforce is like. Your child should never view anything that is paying them, as a job. A job is close to a chore, which most kids hate doing anyway. They should understand that they are now in the career world. They should understand like I've already mentioned, that an employer is AN INVESTMENT INTO THEIR CAREER. You should teach them to stay clear of their peers who don't care about their job in the workforce. These kids are often teaching your child not to care and that not caring is cool. You also want to help your child keep up with how much they are earning. It is very cool for them, after a certain time, to look back and see how much money they have had in their hands during their career while in school. When they add that up and see figures like 8-10k, it sends a strong message of what's to come.

Your child's time during these years is more valuable than yours. You might be saying "what?". But your child has more responsibilities than you think they do. In the 11th grade I wrote a play called "The Young and the Drugless". I stood up and read it to the class. Of course, in the beginning scene there was a student doing drugs, and as I was reading I fell to the floor. I started shaking and blood was coming from my mouth. If I remember correctly, I was having a full convulsive seizure and the class started clapping for my Oscar-like performance. I remember coming to in a wheelchair being rushed down the hallway. Several students shouting my name, some even running along with the wheelchair to ask if I was ok. I couldn't remember most of them and at that point was having trouble even remembering who I was. I eventually arrived at the hospital and later that evening after an MRI and Cat scan I do remember the conversation I had with my doctor. He said they couldn't find anything wrong with me, but asked if I was worried about anything? I told him no, other than school stuff. What kind of school "stuff" are you referring to? Well, I said, I was

- ✓ Up all night studying for a chemistry test that I was sure I'd barely pass. I couldn't make tutoring because of band rehearsal. But I promise I had studied so much after work, after band practice, during the 20-minute break I took to stuff dinner down, and during the much-needed Arsenio Hall show that I never miss. Tears flowing, I was crushed that I had given all the hours between 10pm – 4 or 5am to study and was just not retaining the information. Only to get back up at 7am to make the bus at 7:35am. It was cool because I could get a quick 20-minute nap during that bus ride.

✓ But that wasn't a big deal because I also got to take cool naps in History and the 2 different band periods I had. But wait, then there was the UIL marching contest, oh yea I also had to practice for my solo at UIL.

✓ Then there was the early meeting for SWAT to go over the play.

✓ That's when I remembered that I had missed work and wondered if anyone had called my job. Tears flowing again.

✓ Oh, yeah, I also need to go cut my grandmother and uncle's grass so I can make $20 to help fund my band trip. It's $350 and I haven't been able to work because of band. So, on Sunday I need to go out there and do that.

✓ Wait what day is it, I said. Had to make sure I didn't miss my ability to play timpani at Gerry Glanville's (Houston Oiler Head Coach) Coaches radio show on 610 sports talk. I am the timpani roll you hear at the beginning of this show. Thanks to my wonderful band director Mr. Willis.

✓ Of course, there was also the Ambassador club meeting that I had to run because we were preparing for our annual Halloween party at Piney Point Elementary.

✓ Oh, don't forget the donate a dime campaign from the Yoruba Young Minority Men's club so that we could purchase toiletries for the homeless.

✓ Crap also my Geometry test is tomorrow.

✓ Oh, did anyone call my girlfriend she's mad that I have the marching contest and can't take her to the Halloween dance.

As parents, it becomes easy for us to forcefully get our kids to just step it up. Studying after 9-10pm doesn't allow them to retain information well. They've often been up at that point, about 18 hours. But your communication right now is so important as it affects how they will perform. They can be very mediocre if you allow them to spread themselves thin. A 16/17-year old employee who is considered an A or B player in the workplace will be used as such. Some inexperienced managers will allow A and B players to be over used, and yet allow C/D/F players to get away with things unimaginable. It is important that you teach your child how to communicate with their managers. YOU should not ever, I repeat NEVER speak on behalf of your child. If you have ever gone into a job and asked for an application or told a manager that your child needs a job, be sure you do not go with your child to apply. This is the biggest sign that your child is not ready to enter the workforce. I've been very careful to describe first what your child's responsibility is, prior to talking to you about the mangers who are causing people to leave their jobs. Your child should understand that holding in their frustrations can cause a very uncomfortable workplace environment for them, but that running to the manager to complain about what other people are doing is often a sign that your child is not willing to do "a little extra". They would be better noticed if they can multitask and willing to do a little more than their peers. This willingness to help will be viewed as someone who is doing things because of who they are and not for what they want you to think they have become. They should also know that having a conversation about someone else's performance will never help solve **their** frustrations. They should always concentrate on doing their job well. Once they learn the employer's chain of command, they should follow that. As I stated earlier, some inexperienced managers may let this go on, however, once they learn that your child is aware, it forces them into a decision. The managers must decide if they are going to let it continue, or if they are going to do something about it. The next time this happens to your child, the conversation may be a little different. "Mr. Jordan, we spoke about this before, but Terri is not closing her section again. Did you talk to her? It is really frustrating to me." This sends another message to the manager. Now this is a point where they are not doing their job, and it's effecting the workplace environment. Depending on the chain of command, there is often an anonymous number that you can call, but in most cases, there are other supervisors that can be approached about the situation. Please remember that most companies do not tolerate this kind of management. But they can't fix problems that they don't know exist. Threatening managers or immediately calling corporate is never the answer. Corporate still allows the General Manager to do the investigation, unless he or she is mentioned in the investigation. Most jobs utilize progressive discipline. Even your child will make mistakes. So, your child should never develop the mentality that they are going to get someone fired, or they are going to call corporate because a manager made them mad. Be honest about what's going on, and do your job well. That's the recipe. There are different levels of management but there is always someone in the organization with an answer to your issue or the antidote to any cancers that exist within the organization. Your job as a parent is to first make sure your child looks in the mirror at their performance, making sure that their issue isn't associated with any jealousy or an attempt at revenge, and that they are following the proper channels as set

by the employer,

Chapter Four

What is HR and how does it relate to my child?

The HR department at most companies have worked extremely hard to cover every possibility. They have spent countless hours on your child's possible benefit packages, be it good or small, and they even made a way for your child to potentially earn some paid time off. Not to mention they are the ones responsible for making sure your child gets PAID!!!

Oh, ___no, my child was written up for being late___! What do I do? You should have a conversation with your child about being at work on time. Sometimes this happens. But most young employees are not versed in the latest HR jargon, which changes as laws change, and different legislation is passed. But it is important that if you have a child in the workplace **that you read and discuss the employee handbook.** This is the bible of how the people that created the company have signed off on how they want it to operate. As we discussed in the last chapter, there are situations where some managers are young and inexperienced. For this reason, I encourage you to discuss this with your child, because this handbook is no different from the bible, only knowing part of it, can get you into some seriously confusing situations. Some of the sections that are important for a young employee to understand is the attendance policy. The policy for missing shifts and being tardy. Also, the company's break policy, and the difference between part time and full time, etc. As a parent, you should understand some pretty important topics such as whether your child will be receiving medical benefits and if they can earn paid time off. Discuss How many dependents they are claiming on their W4, and if there is life insurance, who they are putting as their beneficiary. This chapter is certainly not to teach you HR, it's simply to point out some of the main things that I feel several parents and young employees tend to miss out on. Some of them eventually earn paid time off, but often never use it.

Managers who are holding employees accountable will, in fact, utilize a progressive discipline approach to send a message to the staff that certain things will not be tolerated. I remember catching 2 buses, and eventually a cab to arrive at my job where the manager was sitting by the time clock with a pad of consultation reports getting signatures. Amazing as it seems, Mr. Carter hardly ever had anyone late for his shifts. But that day, was my turn to sign my very first one. I signed it, and went on to my shift. A friend of mine behind me, fought and refused to sign it. I eventually made Senior Manager for this company, and my friend is still waiting tables somewhere, I believe. My point is, if you truly understand the handbook and have discussed the discipline policies with your child, they will not be surprised when they are applied. In fact, how your child behaves during the consultation with the management team is often a reflection of the direction their career will follow. If you hold your child accountable to doing chores, keeping his room clean, and respecting your curfew, why wouldn't his job have the same, if not higher expectations considering they are paying him? Your child's behavior is often reflected the same way at home as it is at work. But I will let you in on a little secret. The way your child's friends (circle of friends) behave is often how your child behaves away from home. Just as the General Manager will always see the best behavior, your child will always show you their best behavior, or at least attempt to show you their very best. Now how his friends react, and behave with adversity and change is likely how your child tries to behave when he is with his circle of friends. Look no further than their social media pages. Especially Apps like Instagram, Marco Polo, Snap Chat, and several other apps that allow your kids to communicate much easier than we did as children.

You will often see how these kids are dressing, what type of language they are speaking, and even how they are not dressing. These are things that employers are not allowed to consider during the interview process, but you can gain access to your child's social media page. I strongly recommend that your child try not to work with his friends. Even if your child is a good employee, or has a friend that is a good employee, they will often refer their friends because people in our industry are ALWAYS looking for staff. But the more friends you have working together, the harder it is for them to concentrate on doing their job well. It often becomes a social gathering, versus your child trying to be the best that they can be in their career. Now don't get me wrong, if your child has a great circle of friends, and they are all solid rock stars, you will know right away their ability to work together.

Also, remember that these years are prime puberty years. Keeping with what I said about always seeing the best that your child must offer, I can't begin to tell you the number of young ladies and gentlemen that allow their performance to plummet during a relationship. They are OFTEN not able to function anymore. They are at work on their off days watching their boyfriend/girlfriend work. They stick around and wait for them to get off. Some young ladies even start to have issues with other young ladies that look at or approach their boyfriend. Some boyfriends often are willing to fight, threaten or put them in possible criminal situations trying to protect a young lady in the work place. Like your child not working with their friends, working with a girlfriend or boyfriend is often a great recipe for disaster in the workplace. If your child is always at the job, review his or her check stub. If they are only being paid for 15-20 hours a week, and you don't see them until

10pm every night, you need to have a conversation. Surely if you are having the right conversations with your child ahead of time, most of these situations are simply worse case scenarios. Other big topics that are often missed, as it relates to HR, is that it's not a male to female issue. Some of these young men are also being harassed and it often gets swept under the rug, because most-young men will tolerate being harassed by a female employee. But male to male and female to female harassment is not uncommon, and some young employees are afraid to discuss the situation with management because of what others may think. It is often used as jokes, or the emphasis "JK" after a text. Just kidding does not negate vulgar or otherwise hurtful rhetoric. It's simply a way to say something to gauge a reaction and learn how to precede from there. Again, it is key to be clear about what your child is offended by and situations like this must be reported for it to be addressed. Just like I will tell you that most customers don't complain, they just don't return. Most A and B employees don't complain they just quit. So, if your child is ready to just quit a job they love, you should encourage them to talk about the situation or at least learn if the company has an anonymous tip line to address their concerns. Never allow your child to just quit a job without asking or probing. Mainly because closing the door on a company forever is simply not a good idea. But if there is something going on at work, most great companies will want to know. Even if you decide to move on, they should at least give the investor into their career an opportunity to correct the issue, or correct your child. When some people think about HR they immediately relate it to sexual harassment which is a very small portion of what they do. In fact, most sexual harassment issues are handled swiftly and without incident unless you are dealing with an inexperienced management team, or a management team that simply doesn't care. Again, this is not a lesson on sexual harassment, but it comes down to unwelcome sexual advances, requests for sexual favors, and other verbal or physical harassment of a sexual nature. The one thing that you should discuss with your child is that social media hasn't necessarily made it into some handbooks or topics at orientation. However, things sent over snap chat, Marco Polo, and some of these other apps can absolutely get your child caught up in inappropriate situations at work. Harassment does not have to be sexual either. It can be vulgar, offensive, or just "uncomfortable". There are also other employees who are well versed in the hot buttons of certain employers and if they ever become jealous or angry at your child they will use whatever they can to cause your child problems. So many people associate nude photos being sent by young ladies, but surprisingly there are several young men who have zero problem with shooting a picture in the buff to someone they feel they can trust. But in most cases, it only takes an argument or a break up for these photos to start floating around via social media or reported to management at work. You should also remain mindful that there are absolutely adults working with your child. Some of which are very knowledgeable of how to approach these kids. This is often and most likely not seen by the employer, as in most cases, they know to keep this away from work. Also as an employer, we do not get to choose who your child communicates, has lunch, or attends a party with outside of the work place. This is a conversation you need to have with your child to ensure that they are making great decisions. Alcohol is often served at these parties, along with other extra-curricular activities. The easiest thing to know is that someone offering a promotion to an employee for a sexual act is wrong. But also, things like taking managers gifts, lunch, and other favors such as working off the clock is a sign that you may need to speak with your child, BUT NOT HIS MANAGER. These things are often never allowed by a company. The number one thing your child needs to understand about their safety in the workplace is that if someone says or does something that makes them feel uncomfortable, they need to be clear in letting them know that they are not only offended, but also ask that they not do it again. Things like accepting a hug every day, or comments that grow from "You look nice" to "Hey sexy" often lead to other conversations that take an unfortunate direction. Be sure that your child understands to simply be clear that they are offended and not use words like "I'm flattered" or "I have a boyfriend". because I promise they don't care anything about your boyfriend, and being flattered is absolutely saying to them you like what they said or did. Even if you follow that up with "but no thanks", in their mind, it's just a matter of time until your child sees things their way. So again, help set the foundation of your child's career, mainly by helping them understand the expectation of the company, and the fact that the employer has invested in their career. Live by the Golden Rule (Do unto others, as you would like done unto you.) For that to work, as a parent, you must set the foundation for your child's future. Always teach them "There is no "I" in team, but there is a "U" in US." (Derwin Jordan) Together, you will be there to support them, but they must be willing to put in the work. This will once again have you helping your child and *people be great again!*

Chapter Five

Your child the hired hook up!

Another huge part of the handbook, and the second biggest retention killer amongst teenage workers is THEFT. I've heard the phrase "Misery loves company" repeatedly. This is the reason it is so important for you to teach your child about integrity. The one thing that my father drilled into my brain was that INTEGRITY was the one thing that I possessed that no one in the world could take from me. He said it was the one thing from a decision stand point where I was the sole proprietor. He said that I would have to make a conscience decision to give it up. Most theft occurring in companies is often passed down the line, believe it or not, much like in prison. Once an employee figures out a way to beat the system, they can't wait to share it with a friend. Also, as soon as your child gets the cool theater job, or a place that sells fun, they are often under a ton of pressure to provide their friends with "the hook up". Surprisingly enough, family also plays a vital role in getting young employees to do more than they can do. Again, all of this is laid out clearly in the employee handbook. Even if it's putting an extra slice of cheese on a burger, if it's not paid for, it's theft. Letting your friends into the back door of the movie, even though they are sitting in the front row where no one ever sits, is theft. Most of these places have incentives for your child to enjoy. There are often off peak times designed for them to enjoy the facilities. But, especially family, will encourage and even pressure them to give others the ability to play or eat for free. Make sure your child understands the consequences of their actions. As I guarantee when your child loses their job for giving away a free burger, the person that received the free burger will be incognito when your child needs a few dollars in the future. You should encourage your child to know about employee of the month programs, sales contest incentives, and many other benefits or perks that the company offers. These are things that you should be aware of to help celebrate their hard work and extra, extra, curricular efforts. Particularly if you have an A or B player as a child, understand their work load. Provide support and not ammunition for hostility. Teach them to expect and demand to be held accountable. Check to see if they are having fun at work. If they are dreading to go to work, it's likely not the job for them. AND THAT'S OK! This is the time that will allow them the ability to form opinions on what they want to do long term. Teach them to submit a two weeks-notice in writing. Make sure that they are on their best behavior during this notice and that they could possibly return to work during the summer or during certain holidays. Never burn a bridge that you may have to cross again in the distant future.

In closing.......

Make sure they LOVE what

they do!

My high school career was spent knowing, without a shadow of a doubt, that I was going to eventually become a band director. Especially once I made Drum Major in the 11th grade.   Being president of a club, getting promoted from regular employee to crew leader at the age of 17 at Chick Fil A, had nothing to do with the career I was to have as an illustrious maestro of music one day. After all, band was what I LOVED doing. I mean, my father Fred M. Jordan III, wrote scores for movies, worked with the great Johnny Nash, and co-wrote the Tokyo Music Award for the song Belle by Al Green. Surely MY music career was going to be a HUGE success? However, once I made it to my music theory class at Texas Southern University, my professor asked me to come play and sing a note in front of the class. Haven't you had piano lessons? He asked. No sir, I said. As drum, major in high school you never took any additional music theory classes in drum major camp? He pleaded. No sir, I said, I had to work during the summer, before I graduated, I became the assistant night manager at Chick Fil A. I never went to those camps etc. Well if you can't sing this note, he sighed, how were you able to tune the band as drum major? Oh, I can read music as the day is long, but for tuning the band, I used this little box that I had the horn players blow into and I would just tell them if they were flat or sharp. We continued with the class, and afterwards he broke the news to me that just knowing how to play percussion (drums), and only being able to read music, at this level, would make for an almost impossibility to become a band director. Didn't mean you would have to give up your band scholarship, but it was very likely that you would have to choose a new major. After careful consideration of my ability to speak to anyone, Public Relations would be my major of choice, with a minor in communications. After a few more practices in band, I had to make another very hard decision in my college career. Being the Drum Major in my High School band had limited my playing time on the snare drum to almost nothing. Where I was once the best in my craft, I no longer had the ability to play for long periods of time. Also after cutting my thumb open with an electronic knife down to the tendon, I could no longer bend the thumb on my right hand and holding a drum stick after a certain amount of time in that hand became very painful. This meant that I was no longer able to play the most coveted drum in the band. To the cymbal section I marched. Where most of us assumed those were the guys who could never quite play the other instruments very well. At least that was what I thought, until I had to jump and crash the cymbals between my legs, twirl them and do splits. I found there was nothing easy about playing cymbals at Texas Southern. However, I was never satisfied not playing something that I used to do so well. I eventually went on to play the Bass Drum, but soon lost interest in marching and was now trying to figure out how I would pay for college, if I didn't play in the band any longer. While all of this was going on, I landed what would eventually be the University of my career. Not only would I find a major that I loved, but I would be allowed to work with the best instructors in the business. As my interest dwindled in the band, I was forced to decide between band at Texas Southern or this other University that would not only allow me to major in the right career, but continue the very foundation that was set by Chick Fil A. After receiving a new band director at Texas Southern, I was told that if I couldn't attend both rehearsals, that I would not be able to keep my $300 a semester scholarship. Oh, did I mention that this said "other" University was not only NOT going to charge me to attend, they would PAY me to be there. I was very torn, as everyone will tell you that going to college is the right thing to do. And I do still believe that. But it is extremely important that you know what your child LOVES to do, because when they love doing it, sometimes they do it without knowing. I sat down with my uncle Buford. This University that I'm speaking of was Dave and Buster's University. When I started working with them, they had 3 stores, by the time I went on to my third company they had 58. When I was contemplating leaving college, Dave and Buster's was telling me that it was a great possibility that I could get promoted if I just opened my *availability*. (See that word again?) So, my uncle and I started to look up salaries of people in different fields, starting with band directors. Then we started to look up people in the field that was in the business I had been in since High School. There were some regular plain old restaurant managers making 10-20k more than the highest paid high school band director. Some General Managers, Regional, and Area managers were making 6 figures. Some of these people were working at very uncool (if you ask some of today's youth) places like McDonald's, Taco Bell, and other fast food restaurants. Yet as kids, we laughed at the guy flipping fries. At Dave and Buster's, I started as a guy calling the horse races on the microphone. I think I interviewed with them about 3 times before I finally got in. They were so busy at the time, that if I didn't get yes that day, I'd make sure I wore a different suit until I got in. The 3rd time was a charm. I was interviewed by the business manager Kim Martinez. She didn't normally do interviews, but was called to help with the overwhelming number of applicants. I can't begin to tell you how glad I am that I stayed on course with them. I can still remember the time I recorded how many times I said the horse name "Mama Michelle". 1042 times one Saturday. No one ever wanted to work *D&B Downs* *(The horse racing game where you roll balls into a hole to make your horse move.)* and I would come in and ask for it. They didn't know this but it was because you got to keep your drink at your station and I loved Dr. Pepper more than Forrest, Forrest Gump did. Once my supervisor LaVecia Brookins saw me on her shift, she would sometimes just point to *D&B Downs* as I turned the corner. I would smile and grab my mic. My uncle told me that I had one common denominator amongst anything that I've touched. I looked at him, and he looked at me amazed that I didn't see it. We started to discuss some of the things that I started to learn even before getting my first job. Starting with discipline. As a band geek, as we were often called, we learned the importance of being on time. Working hard, and always making sure you looked good doing it. Being Drum Major, President, Secretary, crew leader, etc. all pointed to being a LEADER. Dave and Buster's was starting to take off. They landed themselves on the NASDAQ and started opening 5 stores a year. Unable to keep up with promoting internally they started to bring on managers from the outside. Regional, Area, and even some VP's were leaving their jobs to come and be just regular managers. At a very young age I first worked with a big sister in Felecia Mays Corbin, who taught me to simply be a sponge. She told me to absorb as much knowledge from everyone that I could. Keep the good, and learn from the bad. So, when your child tells you something that they know a manager is doing wrong, applaud them for learning what not to do when they get to that level. One of the biggest mistakes some young employees make is taking for granted the opportunities to learn and grow. The more knowledge I soaked in, the higher up the ladder I climbed. I spoke up for myself, I asked questions when I didn't know, and I always came in with the attitude that I was going to be the best in the building. I eventually held roles as Assistant General

Manager, Special Event Sales Manager, Senior Manager, Bar Manager, Acting General Manager of the newly acquired Jillian's location, and worked in every department in the company as an hourly employee. Over 14 years with them, I had the ability to grow and learn so much about my field, and I learned from some of the best people. I watched so many people just give up for little things. But I also saw people like Russel Jones, and Toby Brown who are still there today celebrating over 20 plus years at the same job. You don't do that unless you love what you do and you work for a company that Loves You. You do that by earning RESPECT, and giving your all 100% of the time. Don't allow your child to treat their job as a chore. Make them invest as much, if not more, than the employer that is investing in them. Being the best you can be, is not a switch to flip. You must do it because that's who you are, not because that's who you claim to be. It has always been important to me both as a father and a manager that people understand that I am who I claim to be. There is a lot going on in the world today from a political stand point, but we must look at ourselves and ask are we trying to be great because that's who we are or because someone wanted us to be. Your child working during high school is a major commitment, especially with the amount of homework kids take home today. It is an extremely intense responsibility added to the pressure of school. If your child is not able to handle it, help he or she recognize it and then leave the company in a professional manner. But invest not only money into your child's career, invest your time with them. Not their managers. There are several chain restaurant's popping up right now with plans to open multiple units. Right now, is the time to get in them on the ground floor. Do your research, communicate with your child, and challenge them to be the best. Being great is a journey and not a destination. Therefore, we must get up every day with the mentality that as parents, we will help our children be Great Again, TODAY!

 Remember;

THERE IS NO "I" IN TEAM, BUT THERE IS A "U" IN US!!!!

Thank you for your time, Derwin C. Jordan.

www.ingramcontent.com/pod-product-compliance
Lightning Source LLC
Chambersburg PA
CBHW071811170526
45167CB00003B/1263